global eWorkbook

Contents

Global eWorkbook at a glance

The *Global* eWorkbook combines the best of both worlds: everything you would find in a printed Workbook for home study and multimedia resources to enhance revision and ongoing learning.

The *Global* eWorkbooks are mainly intended for self study or home study. They contain a set of resources to support and enhance the material in the Coursebook. The eWorkbook can be used with your computer or you can save some of the material and use it with other devices (for example, mp3 players).

If you prefer to work on paper you can print your work.

When you launch a level of the *Global* eWorkbooks you will see the following options:

Where to start?

You can start by going to help  or by reading this booklet.

If you want to have a clear overview of the whole content you should select the Contents Map icon.

You can see all the resources linked to each of the units, and you can view them either by type or by the recommended order in which you should use them.

You can see the result of the last self-check test you have done.

You can export your Markbook and share it with your teacher if you want to.

You can see at a glance what resources you have already accessed.

Contents Map | **Markbook** | **Test Results**

Unit 1
Unit 2
Unit 3
Unit 4
Unit 5
Unit 6
Unit 7
Unit 8
Unit 9
Unit 10

Language practice

Grammar 1	Auxiliaries	
Grammar 2A	Review 1: Present tenses	
Grammar 2B	Review 1: Present tenses	
Grammar 2C	Review 1: Present tenses	
Grammar 3A	Review 2: Future tenses	
Grammar 3B	Review 2: Future tenses	
Vocabulary 1A	Predicative adjectives	
Vocabulary 1B	Predicative adjectives	
Vocabulary 2A	Time phrases: *soon*	
Vocabulary 2B	Time phrases: *soon*	
Vocabulary 3	The suffix *-able*	
Vocabulary 4	Metaphors for illness	
Reading	First impressions	
Reading	First impressions Answer Key	
Listening	Family past	
Pronunciation 1	Emphasising	
Writing	A letter to keep in touch	
Writing	A letter to keep in touch Answer Key	

Listen on the move

In Conversation	At work

Sort by: ○ Sequence ● Type

Global eWorkbook Upper Intermediate Markbook   Unit 1

Language Practice

Grammar 1	Auxiliaries	7/9
Grammar 2A	Review 1: Present tenses	8/10
Grammar 2B	Review 1: Present tenses	4/8
Grammar 2C	Review 1: Present tenses	0/7
Grammar 3A	Review 2: Future tenses	6/8
Grammar 3B	Review 2: future tenses	0/8
Vocabulary 1A	Predicative adjectives	6/6
Vocabulary 1B	Predicative adjectives	3/6
Vocabulary 2A	Time phrases: soon	0/8
Vocabulary 2B	Time phrases: soon	8/8
Vocabulary 3	The suffix –able	4/6
Vocabulary 4	Metaphors for illness	0/5
Reading	First impressions	done
Listening	Family past	
Pronunciation 1	Emphasising	2/6
Writing	A letter to keep in touch	
Total		**48/95**

Listen on the Move

In Conversation	At work	done
Useful Phrases	Metaphors for illness	
Useful Phrases	Questions about your family	
Vocabulary Builder	Adjectives	done
Vocabulary Builder	Predicative adjectives	
Vocabulary Builder	Future time expressions	
Vocabulary Builder	Suffix –able	

Watch

Video	Visiting time	done
Video	Visiting time Worksheet	done
Video	The travel writer	
Video	The travel writer Worksheet	

12th October 2011   Page 1

Language Practice

LANGUAGE PRACTICE

The Language Practice section includes activities that provide consolidation of the language presented in the Coursebook. It includes practice of all language skills: grammar, vocabulary, pronunciation, reading, listening and writing.

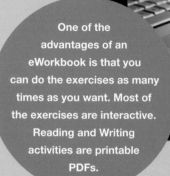

global

UPPER INTERMEDIATE   eWorkbook

LANGUAGE PRACTICE

BY UNIT

| Unit 1 | Unit 2 | Unit 3 | Unit 4 | Unit 5 |

| Unit 6 | Unit 7 | Unit 8 | Unit 9 | Unit 10 |

BY SKILL

| Grammar | Listening | Pronunciation |

| Reading | Vocabulary | Writing |

One of the advantages of an eWorkbook is that you can do the exercises as many times as you want. Most of the exercises are interactive. Reading and Writing activities are printable PDFs.

You can navigate the material by unit or by language skill. If you choose to work by unit, you will be taken to a list of all the activities related to that particular unit.

If you choose to work by skill, you will be taken to a list of all the different activities related to that particular skill.

global

UPPER INTERMEDIATE   eWorkbook

LANGUAGE PRACTICE

UNIT 1

Grammar 1	Auxiliaries
Grammar 2A	Review 1: Present tenses
Grammar 2B	Review 1: Present tenses
Grammar 2C	Review 1: Present tenses
Grammar 3A	Review 2: Future tenses
Grammar 3B	Review 2: Future tenses
Vocabulary 1A	Predicative adjectives
Vocabulary 1B	Predicative adjectives
Vocabulary 2A	Time phrases: soon
Vocabulary 2B	Time phrases: soon
Vocabulary 3	The suffix -able
Vocabulary 4	Metaphors for illness

When you choose an activity practising grammar, vocabulary, listening or pronunciation you will be taken to a screen like this one.

| Unit 1 | Vocabulary 4 (Extend your vocabulary) | Metaphors for illness |

Complete the text about falling ill with the words in the box.

| attacks | defences | lose the battle | fight | victim |

In winter elderly people are more likely to fall [ ] to illnesses like common colds and flu. These can then be quite serious as old people's natural [ ] are not as strong as those of younger people. Although their bodies try to [ ] illness they often [ ] So, rather than trying to cure old people it is better to try and prevent such [ ]

| Check answers | Show answers | Try again |

Whichever way you work you will always be able to access the following resources: Dictionary, Grammar Help, Word Lists and Writing Tips.

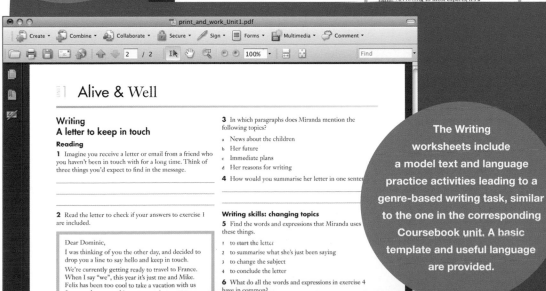

You will be able to check your answers, show them etc. If an audio file is needed, you will be able to click on the relevant icon and play it.

To do a Reading or Writing activity you will need the free program Acrobat Reader.

Reading texts relate to the topic of the Coursebook unit and are information-rich. As well as comprehension questions there are exercises relating to language content (vocabulary/grammar). There is one reading text for each unit. You can also open the answer key as a separate document.

The Writing worksheets include a model text and language practice activities leading to a genre-based writing task, similar to the one in the corresponding Coursebook unit. A basic template and useful language are provided.

Unit 1 — Vocabulary 4 (Extend your vocabulary) — Metaphors for illness

Complete the text about falling ill with the words in the box.

attacks   defences   fight

In winter elderly people are more likely to fall ☐ victim ✓ to illnesses like common colds and flu. These can then be quite serious as old people's natural ☐ lose the battle ✗ are not as strong as those of younger people. Although their bodies try to ☐ illness they often ☐ . So, rather than trying to cure old people it is better to try and prevent such ☐ .

Try again   Show answers   ✖ << Menu >>

Unit 1 — Alive & Well

Reading
First impressions

1 Put these items into order of importance when you meet someone for the first time. 1 = most important, 5 = least important.

choice of clothes _____
physical appearance _____
handshake _____
eye contact _____
tone of voice _____

2 Read the article and write the answers to these questions.

1 According to the article, what gives the best impression at a job interview?

2 What has new research in The British Medical Journal shown?

3 What other things did the researchers look at?

3 Write the verbs in the correct form.

First impressions

Do you have a firm handshake? Shaking someone's hand is often the first contact we have with a person and can often be the only physical contact we ever have with him or her. Although it happens very quickly and we probably don't think too much about it, a person's handshake is the first non-verbal clue we have to someone's personality. In the few seconds it takes to shake someone's hand, we often know whether or not we are going to relate to the other person.

There have been several studies into how our handshake can influence our chances of success in life. Research by the University of Iowa in the US discovered that people applying for a job have a much better chance of success with a firm handshake. In fact, the handshake was found to be more important than the person's physical appearance or their choice of clothes.

So what is the best way to shake someone's hand? According to most experts, it's a

---

Unit 1 — Alive & Well

Writing
A letter to keep in touch

Reading

1 Imagine you receive a letter or email from a friend who you haven't been in touch with for a long time. Think of three things you'd expect to find in the message.

2 Read the letter to check if your answers to exercise 1 are included.

Dear Dominic,

I was thinking of you the other day, and decided to drop you a line to say hello and keep in touch.

We're currently getting ready to travel to France. When I say "we", this year it's just me and Mike. Felix has been too cool to take a vacation with us for several years, and is now preparing to go to university in Montreal – he is looking forward to

3 In which paragraphs does Miranda mention the following topics?

a News about the children
b Her future
c Immediate plans
d Her reasons for writing

4 How would you summarise her letter in one senten

Writing skills: changing topics

5 Find the words and expressions that Miranda uses these things.

1 to start the letter
2 to summarise what she's just been saying
3 to change the subject
4 to conclude the letter

6 What do all the words and expressions in exercise 4 have in common?

Print and Work

This section offers a pen-and-paper version of the activities in the Language Practice section, plus downloadable audio tracks when needed. It is designed to suit a different learning style. If you prefer to work away from the computer, this gives you exactly the same as what you would expect in a printed workbook with the added advantage that you only print the pages that you need.

Answer Key

Unit 5 Answers

Grammar 1A
1 won't
2 will
3 won't
4 will
5 will
6 won't
7 will, will

Grammar 2A
1 ✓ Correct
2 ✗ Incorrect. We use used to and not would for a past state.
3 ✓ Correct
4 ✗ Incorrect. When / was ten is a specific time and so we use the past simple.
5 ✓ Correct
6 ✓ Correct
7 ✗ Incorrect. In 2003 is a specific time and so we use the past simple.
8 ✓ Correct
9 ✓ Correct

Grammar 2B
1 knew
2 used to love
3 would help / used to help
4 didn't use to like
5 burned / burnt
6 didn't use to let / wouldn't let
7 used to hate
8 used to spend / would spend

Grammar 3A
1 are
2 getting
3 are
4 get
5 is
6 get
7 I'm

Grammar 3B
1 get
2 was
3 get
4 be
5 was
6 is
7 getting
8 getting
9 was

Vocabulary 1A
1 amazing
2 check up on
3 miraculous
4 challenging
5 exhausting
6 noisy
7 underestimated
8 expensive

Vocabulary 1B
1 bringing up
2 spoil
3 praise
4 nickname
5 tell me off
6 trust
7 discipline

Vocabulary 2
1 middle name
2 unisex name
3 patronymic
4 pseudonym
5 stage name
6 nickname
7 maiden name

Vocabulary 3A
Across
1 delicious
4 sour
5 soggy
6 bitter
Down
1 disgusting
2 crunchy
3 sharp
8 bland

Vocabulary 3B
1 delicious
2 lumpy
3 chewy
4 sharp
5 spicy
6 bland
7 crunchy
8 sticky

Extend your vocabulary 1A
1 close
2 inseparable
3 cracks
4 split
5 attached
6 strong

Extend your vocabulary
1 2a 3h 4

Pronunciation 1
1 Don't be late.
2 You just won't listen, it's so annoying.
3 U Yu will talk back to him.
4 Samantha will help you if you ask.
5 They will ignore what's good for them.
6 Children these days just won't pay attention.

Pronunciation 2A
1 flexible
2 strong
3 depth
4 throughout
5 fifth
6 attempt
7 creative
8 lengths

Pronunciation 2B
1 strong
2 four
3 depth
4 said
5 deaf
6 spread
7 fourth
8 two

Listening
1960s: 1 three meals a day
1970s: 2 international dishes
1960s: 3 frozen meals
1960s: 4 the end of breakfast
2000s: 5 prepared meals
2010s: 6 more snacks

Writing
An autobiographical extract

Reading

1 Answer these questions.
1 Are autobiographies a popular form of literature in your country?
2 Do you enjoy reading autobiographies? Why / Why not?
3 Have you ever considered writing your autobiography? If so, who would you want to read it?

2 Read four tips for writing a biography. Then read an extract from an autobiography. Does it follow the advice in the tips?
1 Choose events that helped to define you as a person
2 If possible, connect events to a recurring theme in your life
3 Be descriptive – help paint a mental picture of events
4 Give details – these will help readers to recall similar events in their own lives

I was always a very timid child and it worried me that I didn't talk enough. Unfortunately, when I did talk, I would usually go very red. Whenever this happened, one unforgiving classmate would lick the end of his finger and reach out towards my cheeks while making a loud hissing sound. This made me feel as if everybody in sight had stopped what they were doing to look at me, though in retrospect, I'm not sure many people really noticed.

At around that time, an incident occurred that totally changed my perspective on keeping quiet. One evening during the holidays my family gathered round the kitchen table to discuss a problem involving some land they owned. Proceedings started off calmly, but soon a heated discussion had developed. It suddenly struck me that my uncle, rather than getting involved, just sat and listened. Hector looked nothing like my father, his brother, and had a huge moustache that drooped at the ends. This made him look permanently sad. He must have remained silent for almost an hour, during which time the others failed to reach an agreement. At that point, they turned to him for an opinion. "We need to sell the land," he said, and then fell silent again. He sounded as if he'd known the right answer all along, and days later the land had been sold. Looking back, I suppose Hector might simply have had nothing more to say, but he certainly seemed like the deep thinking quiet type. For the first time, I realised how powerful silence can be.

3 Who do you think the autobiography was written for? Why?
• For the writer, to help him/her remember things.
• For the general public.
• For future generations of his/her family.

Writing skills (1): Saying when things happened

4 Look at the underlined words and phrases in the extract. Which one(s) refer to or introduce these time expressions?
1 a particular time in the past
2 a time period in which something happened
3 every time something happened
4 two things that happened at the same time
5 one thing that happened immediately after another
6 one thing that happened a short time after another

Writing skills (2): Describing perceptions

5 Match the two parts of these sentences from the extract. Then read it again to check your answers.
1 This made me feel as if
2 Hector looked nothing like
3 This made him look
4 He sounded as if
5 He seemed like
a permanently sad.
b he'd known the right answer all along.
c the deep thinking quiet type.
d my father.
e everybody had stopped what they were doing.

6 Complete the rules with the words below.

subject + verb	adjective	noun phrase

1 look / feel / sound / seem + _____
2 look / feel / sound / seem + like + _____
3 look / feel / sound / seem + as if + _____

Preparing to write

7 Read the Writing task below and think about a moment or event in your life to write about. To help you do this, consider looking at old photos, possessions or diaries and talking to friends and family members. Then decide who your intended audience is (see exercise 3) and follow the tips in exercise 2.

Writing

Write an extract for your autobiography.

Useful language
• I was always …
• It worried me that …
• Whenever this happened, …
• This made me feel as if …
• In retrospect, …
• Looking back, …
• An incident occurred that totally changed my perspective on …
• It suddenly struck me that …
• I realised …

Vocabulary 2B
Time phrases: soon

Read the sentences. Is the speaker optimistic (O) or pessimistic (P)? Circle the correct answer.
1 I don't think it will happen in my lifetime. O / P
2 We'll find out the results any day now. I can hardly wait. O / P
3 Don't worry! The next opportunity will be just around the corner. O / P
4 Clean (2) d_____ water is the first step to eradicating many of these common diseases. O / P
5 It's sure to happen before long. O / P
6 They'll develop a source of cheap energy in the near future. Then everything will be fine. O / P
7 There's absolutely no chance. It's simply wishful thinking. O / P
8 As far as I can see any cure is light years away. O / P
9 Even if they find a cure any benefits are probably a long way off. O / P

Vocabulary 3
The suffix -able

Write a word ending in -able in each gap to complete the text about preventing diseases.

Around the world many children become ill and die every year. Although some of the diseases they die from are (1) _____, almost all of them could be prevented. Clean (2) d_____ water is the first step to eradicating many of these common diseases. However, any supply needs to be (3) r_____ so that people know it will be there when they need it.

Fortunately, there are now many (4) r_____ organisations such as UNESCO, Oxfam and Medicins Sans Frontier working to help provide such things as clean water and (5) r_____ energy to communities around the world who still live in situations that most of us would find (6) u_____.

Extend your vocabulary
Metaphors for illness

Complete the text about falling ill with the words in the box.

attacks	defences	fight	lose the battle	victim

In winter elderly people are more likely to fall (1) _____ to illnesses like common colds and flu. These can then be quite serious as old people's natural (2) _____ are not as strong as those of younger people. Although their bodies try to (3) _____ illness they often (4) _____. So, rather than trying to cure old people it is better to try and prevent such (5) _____.

Listening
Family past

Listen to the conversation and decide if the sentences are true (T) or false (F). Circle the correct answer.
1 Both of the woman's parents came from New Zealand. T / F
2 Her grandparents played music as a hobby. T / F
3 The family left New Zealand to find work. T / F
4 Her mother mentions New Zealand quite often. T / F
5 Suzanne still has close family ties with New Zealand. T / F
6 She's worried that things will be different in New Zealand now. T / F

Pronunciation
Emphasising

You are going to hear two sentences. Listen and underline the word you think the speaker has stressed in the second sentence which contrasts with something the first speaker said.
1 a You can't speak English.
  b I can speak English.
2 a He lives with his girlfriend.
  b He doesn't live with his girlfriend.
3 a They're not from Italy.
  b They are from Italy.
4 a You didn't phone me last night.
  b I did phone you last night.
5 a They were here earlier.
  b They weren't here earlier.
6 a She's been to London.
  b She's never been to London.

Reading
Destructive names

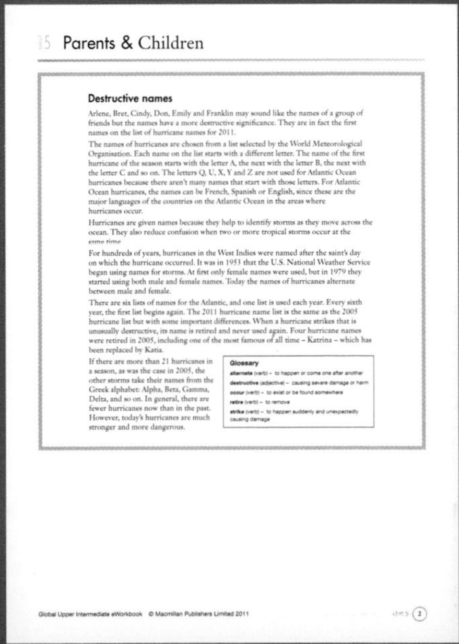

1 What do you think these things have in common? Look the words up in a dictionary to check your answer.

hurricane	cyclone	typhoon

2 What is the worst weather you have experienced? Write five adjectives to describe it and how it made you feel.

3 Read the article and answer these questions.
1 Who chooses the names for the hurricanes?
2 Why are the letters Q, U, X, Y and Z not used?
3 Why are the names French, Spanish or English?
4 Why do they use people's names?
5 What was different about the names between 1953 and 1979?
6 Why is the 2011 list the same as the 2005 list?
7 Why are some names used only once?
8 What's different about hurricanes today?

4 Write the missing words from the final paragraph without looking at the article.
If there are more (1) _____ 21 hurricanes in a (2) _____ was the case (3) _____ 2005, the other storms (4) _____ their names from the (5) _____ alphabet: Alpha, Beta, Gamma, (6) _____ and so on. In (7) _____ there are fewer hurricanes (8) _____ than in the past. (9) _____, today's hurricanes are (10) _____ stronger and more dangerous.

5 Check your answers by looking at the final paragraph of the article.

6 Answer the questions in your own words.
1 How has the media affected your view of hurricanes?
2 What, if anything, do you think towns and cities can do to prevent damage from storms?
3 How do you think the weather has changed in recent years where you live?

Destructive names

Arlene, Bret, Cindy, Don, Emily and Franklin may sound like the names of a group of friends but the names have a more destructive significance. They are in fact the first names on the list of hurricane names for 2011.

The names of hurricanes are chosen from a list selected by the World Meteorological Organisation. Each name on the list starts with a different letter. The name of the first hurricane of the season starts with the letter A, the next with the letter B, the next with the letter C and so on. The letters Q, U, X, Y and Z are not used for Atlantic Ocean hurricanes because there aren't many names that start with those letters. For Atlantic Ocean hurricanes, the names can be French, Spanish or English, since these are the major languages of the countries on the Atlantic Ocean in the areas where hurricanes occur.

Hurricanes are given names because they help to identify storms as they move across the ocean. They also reduce confusion when two or more tropical storms occur at the same time.

For hundreds of years, hurricanes in the West Indies were named after the saint's day on which the hurricane occurred. It was in 1953 that the U.S. National Weather Service began using names for storms. At first only female names were used, but in 1979 they started using both male and female names. Today the names of hurricanes alternate between male and female.

There are six lists of names for the Atlantic, and one list is used each year. Every sixth year, the first list begins again. The 2011 hurricane name list is the same as the 2005 hurricane list but with some important differences. When a hurricane strikes that is unusually destructive, the name is retired and never used again. Four hurricanes names were retired in 2005, including one of the most famous of all time – Katrina – which has been replaced by Katia.

If there are more than 21 hurricanes in a season, as was the case in 2005, the other storms take their names from the Greek alphabet: Alpha, Beta, Gamma, Delta, and so on. In general, there are fewer hurricanes now than in the past. However, today's hurricanes are much stronger and more dangerous.

Glossary
alternate (verb) – to happen or come one after another
destructive (adjective) – causing severe damage or harm
occur (verb) – to exist or be found somewhere
retire (verb) – to remove
strike (verb) – to happen suddenly and unexpectedly causing damage

Listen

This section offers access to all the Listening material in the eWorkbook.
It includes the following:

- Access to the listening activities in the Language Practice section
- Audio material designed to be used 'on the move'

When you select Language Practice you will be taken to the Listening activities in the Language Practice section.

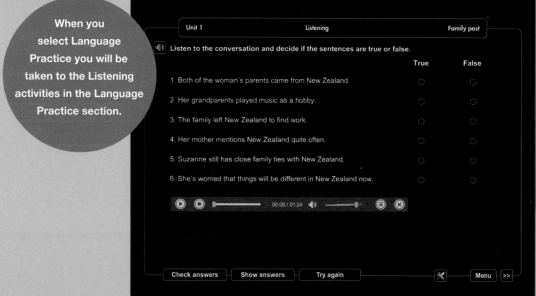

Speech bubbles:
1. "Listen on the Move includes audio material not linked to specific activities, ie different from the listening material in the Language Practice section. There are three types of audio material."
2. "In Conversation contains situational dialogues (eg at a restaurant, taking a taxi). The situations relate to the situations in the 'Function globally' pages in the Coursebook."
3. "Vocabulary Builder contains lists of vocabulary items introduced in the Coursebook which are organised by topic."
4. "Useful Phrases features mini-dialogues that contain the 'Useful phrases' in the Coursebook (eg 'agreeing and disagreeing')."
5. "You can play this material by clicking on play or you can download the files and copy them onto an mp3 player or other devices."
6. "You can also print or download a PDF with the audioscript for all this material."
7. "As its name indicates, this is ideal for learning on the move."

Screen content: global UPPER INTERMEDIATE eWorkbook, LISTEN ON THE MOVE, menu items etc.

Listen on the Move includes audio material not linked to specific activities, ie different from the listening material in the Language Practice section. There are three types of audio material.

In Conversation contains situational dialogues (eg at a restaurant, taking a taxi). The situations relate to the situations in the 'Function globally' pages in the Coursebook.

Vocabulary Builder contains lists of vocabulary items introduced in the Coursebook which are organised by topic.

Useful Phrases features mini-dialogues that contain the 'Useful phrases' in the Coursebook (eg 'agreeing and disagreeing').

You can play this material by clicking on play or you can download the files and copy them onto an mp3 player or other devices.

You can also print or download a PDF with the audioscript for all this material.

As its name indicates, this is ideal for learning on the move.

global
UPPER INTERMEDIATE
eWorkbook
LISTEN ON THE MOVE

In Conversation
Vocabulary Builder
Useful Phrases

- Adjectives
- Predicative adjectives
- Future time expressions
- Suffix -able
- Certainty and truth
- Meanings of right
- The prefix mis-
- ism
- Uesful language
- Natural world collocations
- The sea
- Job suffixes

In an unfamiliar place

A: You know your bag is open, don't you?
B: I'm sorry?
A: Your bag. Be careful with your camera. And your wallet.
B: Oh right. Yes, this city's famous for pickpockets, isn't it? Thank you.
C: I think it's the next station.
D: OK.
D: The next station is Tottenham Court Road. Change here for the Central line. Please mind the gap between the train and the platform.
E: Right. I'm going this way. You should continue down this road as far as the police station. The bus stop's just round the corner.
F: OK. Thanks.
E: Take care.
F: You too. Bye.

In conversation

At work
A: This is Sam. In most cases you'll be working with me but Sam's here if you need him.
B: Apart from Mondays.
A: Oh. That's right. I forgot. Sam's not here on Mondays.
C: Thanks for coming. I don't need an interpreter as a rule but today is an exception.
D: Who is she?
C: The director of the two biggest media companies in Sweden, not counting five new companies.
D: Wow.
C: So in general business is good?
B: By and large, yes.
C: But?
F: Well, except for the shop. Everyone's buying online these days. Jùe know that.

At the dinner table
A: So you think I should stop seeing Jenny?
B: That's not what I said at all. What I meant was you shouldn't see each other so often. Pass the salt.
C: What your father's trying to say is – we never see you.
D: Do you really think his behaviour was acceptable?
E: You must have misunderstood me. I'm just saying that it must be difficult having to be the perfect role model 24 hours a day.
D: In other words, it's OK to do what he did occasionally.
E: Yes. I mean – no.
F: I saw Tom today. He's a nice guy ...
G: Tom? I thought you said he was boring.
F: Did I? If I said that then I didn't mean to say I didn't like him.
G: So you like boring people. Is that why you're with me?
F: OK. Let me put it another way ...

A: So it's
for the li...
B: In effect, yes.
C: This is an interesting survey. Tell us about it.
A: Yes ... well ... our data suggests we need more downtime.
C: Downtime meaning ...
A: Time when we aren't doing anything, not even listening to the radio.
B: It's another cold day for most of the country with heavy rain in many parts. A belt of high pressure is moving towards us so this points to an improvement at the weekend and could even mean some sunshine in parts of England.

At a market
A: Look at that painting. Do you think it's an original?
B: I doubt it, somehow. It's probably a copy.
A: Do you really think so? I'm not so sure. Excuse me!
B: Hi. Can I see that bag?
C: Of course. Here you are. It's the genuine article.
B: Sorry, but I find that a bit hard to believe at that price.
C: My horoscope said I'd be lucky today. Maybe I should buy a lottery ticket.
D: Oh, come on, you don't believe that stuff, do you? It's all nonsense.
C: Well, I suppose it's a bit unlikely that I'll win, but you never know ...

global
UPPER INTERMEDIATE
eWorkbook
LISTEN

Save
Save in: My Computer
Local Disk (C:)
DVD-RAM Drive (D:)
Local Disk (Images) (F:)
matthew beesleys on 'dpu-oxf-data' (G:)
data on 'dpu-oxf-data' (Z:)
File name:
Save
Cancel

Global Upper Intermediate eWorkbook © Macmillan Publishers Limited 2011

Watch

When you select Watch in the main menu you are taken to a screen where all the video clips in the eWorkbook are listed.

You can either watch the videos on your computer or download the files. When you watch the videos on your computer you can select to watch them with or without subtitles.

When you click on 'download' you can copy the files to a selected location. You can download the files in a number of formats, for example for iPod, iTouch, iPhone or other common mobile phones.

You can also download the scripts as a PDF.

1. The travel writer

Length 2:53

Language

Travel vocabulary, describing a place

General information

You can watch the video on your computer or download it onto a portable device. You can choose to watch it with or without subtitles. Use the *pause* and *cursor* controls to watch parts of the video again. There are exercises on this activity sheet to complete before you watch, while you are watching and after you watch.

Important: This is an authentic extract from a BBC TV programme. Don't try to understand every word you hear. Watch and listen for specific information by completing these tasks.

Programme details

This video is from a series called *Culture Shock*. In the series, experts and creative people talk about different forms of art and literature.

Before you watch

1 Complete the descriptions using the words in the box.

expedition	experiences	journals	journey
travelled	went		

1 Herodotus was an ancient Greek historian who lived in the 5th century BC. He _____ widely around the Mediterranean and Black Sea, writing about his

2 Marco Polo (1254–1324) was an Italian merchant who _____ on an epic 24-year _____ to Asia with his father and uncle, writing about their adventures.

3 Captain Robert Scott (1868–1912) was a Royal Navy officer and explorer. His _____ about his final doomed _____ to the Antarctic are famous.

2 What do the three people all have in common?
_____

3 In what ways do you think travel writing has changed in the last 30 years?
_____

While you watch

4 Watch the video and write the names of the places the authors have written about.

1 William Dalrymple
_____

2 Sara Wheeler
_____

5 Watch the video again and complete the sentences with the words in the box.

diverse	enormous	important	intrigued	potent	
ultimate					

1 It is quite literally the most _____ white sheet.

2 You've got to show how _____, how extraordinary, how surprising the world is.

3 The travel writer's job has never been more _____

4 For me (this place) was always the _____ destination for myself as a travel writer.

5 It's a very _____ symbol.

6 In ten years I am only more baffled and more _____ by (this place).

6 Match the quotes in exercise 5 with the writers. Write the numbers.

1 William Dalrymple
_____

2 Sara Wheeler
_____

7 Watch the video again to check your answers to exercises 5 and 6.

8 What do you think the phrases in italics mean? Re-write them in your own words.

1 There are few places in the world that *haven't been well trodden*.

2 Some places that you go to, you feel *you've got the hang of it* in a month or a couple of months.

3 One doesn't have to bother about trying to *get to grips with* the culture because there isn't any.

4 What I wanted to do in *Terra Incognita* was *weave together lots of strands*.

Global Upper Intermediate eWorkbook © Macmillan Publishers Limited 2011

Video Worksheet 1

On the Move

ON THE MOVE

This section includes content also accessible through the Listen and Watch sections offered in one place for ease of access.

When you select this option you are taken to a screen that offers you the option of downloading audio material or video material.

> If you want to access audio material, select Listen on the Move.

> If you want to access video material, select Watch.

global

UPPER INTERMEDIATE

eWorkbook

ON THE MOVE

LISTEN ON THE MOVE

WATCH

> Video files are offered in a variety of formats.

> Audio files are offered as mp3 files.

> In addition, there are PDFs with other assets associated to the audio or video material (eg worksheets to use alongside video clips).

Reference Tools

DICTIONARY WORD LISTS GRAMMAR HELP WRITING TIPS

The *Global* eWorkbook contains powerful Reference Tools to help you with your work.

These tools can be accessed directly from the main menu on the home page or when you are doing an activity.

The Dictionary Tool is a link to the Macmillan English Dictionary Online (you need to be online to access this feature).

Word Lists include the key words that you need to learn in each of the units.

If you select Grammar Help, you can choose from a list of grammar items and get all the relevant information.

When you select Writing Tips you are given a list of topics. Each of them includes a brief explanation on a particular aspect of writing, such as the use of capital letters, spelling, punctuation, paragraphing, etc., followed by a series of multiple-choice questions to ensure that the main points have been understood.

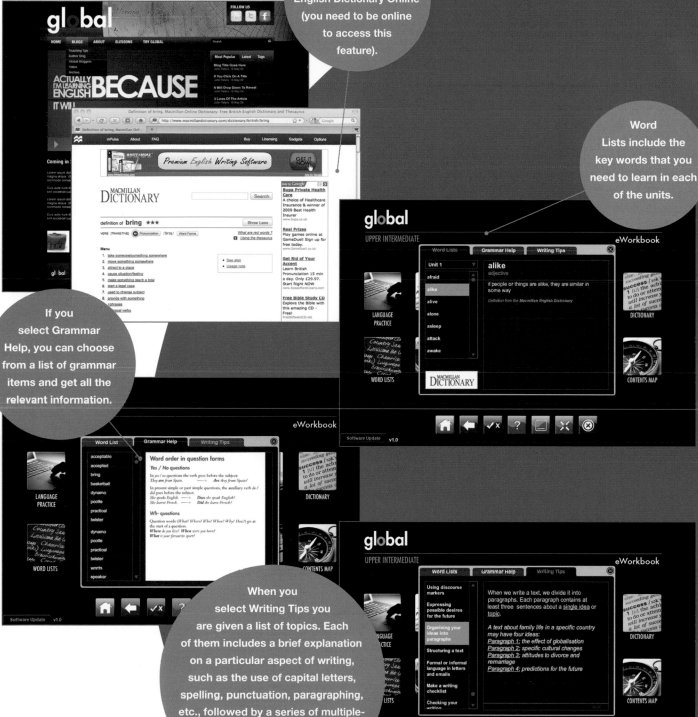

Tests and Portfolio

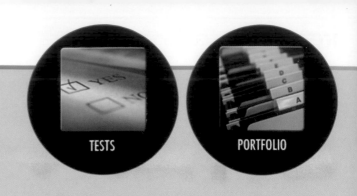

TESTS

PORTFOLIO

You can test yourself at any point using the *Global* eWorkbook. You can set yourself tests either by a set time or a set number of questions.

When you finish the test you will be given a score. Your last three scores will be recorded.

When you select Portfolio in the main menu you are taken to a screen offering information about the Common European Framework, User needs, Language passport and Self-assessment checklists.

Installation instructions

Before you install the *Global* eWorkbook, please make sure that your computer meets the minimum system requirements mentioned below.

To install and run *Global* eWorkbook

Windows

Please select the DVD-ROM drive and double click Install from the Install_Win folder. Follow the on-screen instructions.

Once the installation is complete, an icon will be created on the desktop. To run the application double click the icon.

Macintosh

Please select the DVD-ROM drive and double click Install from the Install_Mac folder. Follow the on-screen instructions.

Once installed, you may wish to drag the application icon from the applications folder to your dock for easy access.

Alternatively, double click the application from the applications folder to launch.

Trouble installing your eWorkbook?

Go to the *Global* website at www.macmillanenglish.com/global

You'll find a section that deals with problems that a small number of users have reported in 'About' under eWorkbook FAQs.

Recommended System Requirements

Windows

Processor: Pentium 4, 3ghz or Intel Core 2 Duo

Hard disk: Minimum 2 GB free, 3 GB free on the system drive

Operating systems: Vista, XP SP2, Windows 7

32 MB Video RAM

2 GB RAM

Audio sound card

DVD drive

Internet Connection (For Registration/live updates)

System administration rights for installation

Macintosh

Intel Core™ Duo 1.33 GHz or faster processor

2 GB RAM

32 MB video RAM

Operating systems: Mac OS X v.10.4 or later

Hard disk: Minimum 2 GB free, 3 GB free on the system Drive

DVD Drive

Internet connection (For Registration/live updates)

System administration rights for installation

Minimum System Requirements

Windows

Processor: Pentium 4, 2ghz or faster

Hard disk: Minimum 2 GB free, 3 GB free on the system drive

Operating systems: Vista, XP SP2, Windows 7

32 MB Video RAM

1 GB RAM

Audio sound card

DVD drive

Internet Connection (For Registration/live updates)

System administration rights for installation

Macintosh

Intel Core™ Duo 1.33 GHz or faster processor

1 GB RAM

32 MB video RAM

Operating systems: Mac OS X v.10.4 or later

Hard disk: Minimum 2 GB free, 3 GB free on the system drive

DVD drive

Internet connection (For registration/live updates)

System administration rights for installation

Macmillan Education
Between Towns Road, Oxford OX4 3PP
A division of Macmillan Publishers Limited
Companies and representatives throughout the world

ISBN 978-0-230-03320-7

© Macmillan Publishers Limited 2011
First published 2011

Written by Robert Campbell, Rob Metcalf, Adrian Tennant, with additional material by Amanda Leigh and Jonathan Coxall
Cover design by Macmillan Publishers Ltd
Design of booklet and worksheets by eMC Design Limited

Cover Credit: Bananastock, Digital Vision, Getty, Image Source

Printed and bound in Spain by Edelvives

2015 2014 2013 2012 2011
10 9 8 7 6 5 4 3 2 1